Charles B. Turrill

Deuteronomy Brown

A Real Estate Transaction

Charles B. Turrill

Deuteronomy Brown
A Real Estate Transaction

ISBN/EAN: 9783337201982

Printed in Europe, USA, Canada, Australia, Japan

Cover: Foto ©Suzi / pixelio.de

More available books at **www.hansebooks.com**

Deuteronomy Brown,

A REAL ESTATE TRANSACTION.

—BY—

CHARLES B. TURRILL,

Author "California Notes," Etc.

1888.

Deuteronomy Brown,

A REAL ESTATE TRANSACTION.

—BY—

CHARLES B. TURRILL,

Author "California Notes," Etc.

1888.

DEUTERONOMY BROWN.

A REAL ESTATE TRANSACTION.

Being of a retiring disposition it is extremely unpleasant to mention myself as frequently as will be imperative in giving a faithful account of the remarkable man, whose name heads this sketch. But as was wisely said by a noted statesman, when running for office, "It is sometimes necessary to exalt yourself in order to elevate the people."

Reared in a quiet New England village, my early life ran as quiet as the mill-pond in which I drowned cats. The prospects of rapidly acquired fortune lured me away from the ancestral kitchen stove, and the aforesaid mill-pond, to try my luck in California, where I was told that fortunes awaited all, and where some overly sanguine individuals declared that every ton of earth contained three thousand pounds of gold. I did not then stop to inquire how many pounds constituted a ton in California, but determined to hasten to the auriferous regions.

I accordingly bid farewell to the adored one, packed my trunk, and took with me a miniature likeness of the charmer of my heart, and a long tress of golden hair. It may appear egotistical, my introducing the information that somebody cared for me, and that I was constant, when from the title of this sketch it would seem that the adventures of an entirely different person were to engross attention. But yet that miniature and that lock of silky hair play an important part in the history of my connection with the character of whom I write. For woman still, rules camp and court and grove, and who's the man who does not love?

I went direct to San Francisco, where I soon succeeded in getting a good position in a large hardware establishment. I had been working there for some two years. Being frugal, I had accumulated a nice little sum, and was thinking of writing to the original of the miniature and asking her to fly to my arms and make happy my lonely, wretched life.

By way of parenthesis, I might remark that condition like mine is always described as "lonely and wretched," and I am too new a hand at literary composition to break down the fence of custom with impunity.

About this time, when I dreamed nightly of my loved one far away, and in my slumbers saw her at my side, in a happy home all our own—as long as I paid the rent— I happened to notice an advertisement in the Sacramento *Record-Union.* This stated that a foothill farm was for sale. Persons desirous of purchasing such a property were advised to address "D. B.," Auburn. immediately.

Had I been at all suspicious I might have interpreted "D. B." to mean "deadbeat." I was not suspicious. I wrote "D. B.," stating a desire to obtain such a place and asking particulars by return mail.

Visions of a productive farm, nestling in some mountain valley—grassy meadows skirting the confines of low, rolling hills, over which at evening came the sounds of lowing herds, tinkling cow-bells and whistling cowboys— good cowboys—appeared to me, as I re-read the advertisement. When I went to bed, and, as usual, placed the tress of golden hair beneath my pillow, my thoughts wandered away from the hardware business, away from nails and spikes, picks and shovels, door-knobs and bar iron; yea, wandered away, and the tress of hair seemed to grow longer and longer and still more long, till it lay like a streak of sunshine on the landscape, stretching over hill and dale, until it enclosed a little paradise of one hundred and sixty acres—my farm!

The next mail brought no answer to my letter. I wondered at the delay. Perhaps I was too late and somebody else had invaded and taken possession of my promised land. Two or three days—long-expectant days—had elapsed since I had written my letter. While I was busy showing a customer some burglar-proof padlocks, an elderly gentleman, dressed in a suit of custom-made clothes, entered the store and was sent by another clerk to me. He waited until I was at leisure, and then handed me a card on whIch was printed

. . . . ,
: DEUTERONOMY BROWN. :
. . . . :

The name was unknown to me, and I intimated as much to the elderly gentleman. He asked if I had not answered an advertisement, and informed me he was "D. B."

Instantly I forgot all about burglar-proof locks. The long tress of golden hair seemed to wind around the elderly gentleman from the foothills and drew him into close fellowship with myself.

He spoke in glowing terms of his farm. The land would raise anything except bread, for which yeast was still required. This seemed a pet joke with "D. B.," accordingly I laughed. Water was abundant—clear mountain streams danced merrily adown the hillsides and sang songs of rejoicing as they sped along. The foothill fruits were celebrated. The means of getting them to market were not excelled. And the climate!— well, now, when you talked of climate that was where any one would have been charmed. Neither too hot nor too cold. None of your frigid mountain climates to chill the marrow in your bones. None of your semi-tropic business, where you lay around in swinging hammocks in a *dolce far niente* style year out and year in; but a climate with a snap and a zest in it—a climate just adapted to active young men, who want to be up and doing, ever striving, ever pursuing.

The title was perfect. It came from the United States, and the United States seemed to be a legitimate squatter. There could be no adverse claimant. The only claimant—the Digger Indian—was dead. He died without heirs.

I was pleased—in fact overjoyed—and closed a bargain at once. It would not do to risk losing such a desirable investment by delay. When I went to my lunch we went to a lawyer's office and had the deed drawn up. The money was paid. I had invested all my savings, and was the happy possessor of a foothill farm, and my next neighbor was D. B.

I could hardly thank my friend enough for his kindness in letting me buy the property. I hardly knew how to address him. D. B. seemed too short and crisp, as it were; rather too familiar with such a generous individual. If I started in at Deuteronomy I was apt to forget his last name after traveling over such an extensive preface —·was in danger of losing the thread of the narrative, so to speak; and might run the risk of offending him by calling him Smith or Jones. But we managed to get on, nevertheless, as I compromised matters by styling him "my friend." It was arranged that my benefactor should take charge of things for the present. I was to pass my vacation, which was not far distant, at my own place.

I paid for the lunch, of course. I felt that I had grown fully six inches in height. I could say *my place!* I seemed to have a tendency to soar a little, and was in constant dread of hitting my head against the ceiling. So, in order to quiet my feelings and be safe, I found it necessary to carry a quantity of railroad spikes in my pockets by way of ballast. Still, I bowed my head every time I passed through a door. "My place!" Oh, joy of joys!

The long days dragged slowly on, and the time for my vacation came at last. My happiness was supreme. The clerks spoke of my changed appearance, but did not suspect the cause. They knew nothing of my purchase. I could not tell them yet. I would get everything ready, and would then write to the original of the miniature, and she would fly to my arms. Then would I sever my connection with the hardware business. Then, and not till then, should they know all. Then would I introduce "my wife," and tell them that I was going to live on "my farm!"

I didn't go to bed the night before my departure. I was to leave on the early train, and did not want to miss the cars. I got my things ready. I would take my gun, as D. B. said there was an abundance of game near my place. I also took a tape measure to measure the rooms for carpets. There was a house on my place. D. B. said it was a picturesque mountain home. I could alter it over a little, so as to make it suit my taste, for the house must be built to suit the man to make a true home. I could put on a wing here, and a bay window there, and a porch here, and year by year could build on more additions as my family increased. I blushed; but saw the beauty of his judgment. And as years rolled by there would be accretions to the old homestead, till it would be a priceless heirloom to hand down to generations yet unborn. Yes; I took a tape-measure!

I was sorry "she" was not to be at my elbow to suggest and help me decide about carpets, and additions and all the little alterations. But I would do the best I could alone. I would not be alone long.

I thought of one thing more, and went to a book store to get a book on "Home Decorations." I went to a store where I was not known. I didn't want anyone to suspect my happiness yet. I bought four books on "Home Decoration." It would be wise to compare different authors' ideas. I also bought two books on Architecture, as applied to country homes. The dealer thought it would be well for me to have two. I also purchased a work on "Landscape Gardening." "Didn't I want a cook-book?" "No, not yet."

I was at the depot three-quarters of an hour early. It is well to be early in going to trains. I bought papers of all the newsboys who came along. I was so happy. What was a little small change at a time like this, when I was going to my place? All my overcoat pockets were filled with morning papers, and I had a bundle of them in my hands also. After I got on the cars an elderly gentleman said to me:

"Young man, I want a *Chronicle!*" I could not be angry with him for taking me for a newsboy. I was too happy, for I was going to my farm, and he was an elderly gentleman, about the same age, I judged, as my benefactor, D. B.

I never saw a train of cars run slower. I asked the conductor several times what the matter was. He answered "nothing" about twenty times, and then ceased to pay any attention to my questions. In my desperation I asked the brakeman. He replied "Nothing," until he got to Sacramento, and after that he only came to the door of the car to call the names of stations, and slammed the door before I could interrogate him. I questioned all the passengers near me, till they either got out, or went into some of the other cars. Even the peanut boy ceased to pass through that car after awhile. My happiness was so great that I was miserable. I doubt not I made others so.

But at last we reached Schooner Gap and I got off. My place was about two miles beyond. I would have to walk that distance. What a relief to be on my feet. I inquired the way more as a means of letting people know I had a place than anything else. As the railroad passed through my land all I had to do was to walk along the track.

It was nearly night when I reached "The Gap," as this station is called in the neighborhood. Leaving my gun and valise with the ticket agent, who owned that portion of the railroad, I continued my pigrimage toward the Mecca of my hopes. It was a pleasant walk in the vanishing sunlight. Steep, pine-clad mountain slopes were growing dusky in the coming gloom. Meditating upon my farm, I wondered if it was on any of the side-hills I beheld. A wagon road was near the railroad track, on which I was walking, and the dust of a summer's accumulation rose in clouds as wagons passed. There were small houses here and there. These seemed to have been built before paint was invented, but appearances are sometimes deceptive. I was surprised at the number of goats I saw. It must be a good country for goats. I have always had an idea that goats were about the last animals created, and that all the perversity on hand, after making hogs, was put into the travesties upon sheep. To avoid passing through a tunnel I had to take a narrow trail on a hill slope. The whole hillside was covered with rocks and brush, and in the middle of the trail stood a goat. He faced me, and evidently intended to continue to do so, and hold the trail. I tried to induce him to give way. No. I even informed him that I owned a farm near by; but that was of no avail. He looked at me as though he had not had the pleasure of meeting me before, and desired to know me should we meet again. I endeavored to convince him that it was impolite to stare at strangers, and not turn out. But he did not look at the matter in that light. So, at last, I left the trail, and stumbled over rocks and through brush till I had traveled around that goat. I thought it best to do so. It might teach him by example better manners.

After reaching the trail again, I looked back; the goat was deliberately walking up the hillside above the path. I was not angry at his goatship—merely annoyed, as I rubbed my bruised shins and felt rents in my clothes.

It seemed I had gone far enough; so, seeing a house near the railroad track, I made my way over rocks and among brush to it, and inquired for Mr. Deuteronomy Brown.

"Do ye want ter see that ould fraud?" asked a lady of Hibernian proclivities, in a shrill voice, that I estimated to be about 200 degrees above zero.

"I would like to find Mr. Deuteronomy Brown," I replied.

"Be yez a sheriff?"

"No, madam; I own a farm, and would like to find Mr. Brown."

"Ye owns a farm, does yez? Shure, an' I'd never thought the loikes of ye owned a farm."

"Can you tell me where I will find Mr. Brown?" I asked again, rather angrily.

"Shure, an' I can; ye'll find the ould fraud at home."

"But, where is that?"

"Where he lives, av course."

"Certainly, madam; but where does he live?"

"On the road to Cold-facts."

"Cold-facts? Oh, I presume you mean Colfax?"

"Av course I do; faith, an' didn't I say that?"

"But how far is it?"

"Shure, an' it's about two miles, an' if that's all ye wanted why didn't ye ax me at onst, an' not kape me waitin'?"

There was a peculiar expression in the lady's eyes which caused me to think that perhaps I had better go on. So, I bade her adieu, and went back to the railroad track.

After traveling some distance further I saw another house off to the left, and went there in search of information.

"Does Mr. Deuteronomy Brown live here?" I asked of a tall, slabsided girl, who came to the door.

"Mam!" she shouted in a Z sharp voice.

"What?" answered another female voice.

"Come here!" shouted the maiden in a higher key

than before, about a Z3 sharp.

"What do you want?" came back from the interior of the house.

"Come here quick!"

"What on earth's the matter with you?"

"Here's a man!"

"Well, what of that?"

I had asked for Mr. Brown three times during the dialogue, and from the latter portion of the girl's remarks began to think I had reached my destination.

"He's a stranger!" continued the girl to the unseen female.

"Where did he come from?"

"Don't know."

"Well, can't you ask?"

I volunteered the information that I journeyed from San Francisco, and asked again if Deuteronomy Brown lived there.

"He says he came from San Francisco."

"Well, I'll be there in a minute."

I waited fully a quarter of an hour, while there were mysterious sounds in the house, and while the mountain maiden at my side took an inventory of my clothing. I was tired, but there was no place to sit. I rested my weight on one leg, and asked if Mr. Brown lived there; then changed the weight on the other leg, and asked where Mr. Brown lived.

To my repeated questions the mountain siren answered:

"Mam'll be here pretty quick."

"Mam" at length arrived, and the delay was explained. She had changed her dress and combed her hair and powdered her face. How much other reconstruction she had undergone while I had been impatiently waiting I am not prepared to state. These alterations were self-evident.

"How do you do, madam?"

"How air ye, sir?"

"Does Mr. Deuteronomy Brown live here?"

"No, he don't," rather snappishly.

"Can you tell me where he does live?"

"I suppose I could," still more snappishly.

"Will you be so kind?"

"He lives up the road," more snappishly than ever.

"Can you tell me how far?"

"I s'pose I could!" words bitten into fragments.

"Can I trouble you to do so?"

"Ain't got no time to bother 'bout no Browns!" words bitten into smaller fragments.

"Will you kindly tell me how far it is to Mr. Brown's?"

"Two miles!!" verbal explosion—door slams—"mam" disappears—darkness reigns.

Three things were evident. The Browns didn't live in that house. They lived two miles further. (Mem.:—country people are not good judges of distances, as it was two miles from the house of the Irish lady, which was at least a mile behind me, as well as two miles from the railroad station.) The ladies I had just talked with were not on friendly terms with the Browns.

I went back to the railroad track. It was now quite dark. - I was tired and was getting discouraged. Nothing but eagerness to get to my farm would urge me on.

I followed the track until I thought I must be pretty near Omaha. I had given up all thought of finding Brown that night. I must be miles beyond his place. I was only looking for a house where I might stop for the night. Trudging along, I saw another light on the left. I decided to try my luck again. Experience had taught me a lesson. So I determined to use diplomacy, as I wanted a place to sleep, and did not want to ruin my prospects by inquiring for a family that did not seem popular.

Fortunately a wagon road crossed the railroad track. I didn't have brush and stones to contend against in going toward the house, where a flickering light was shining through the window.

I reached the house and knocked. I was too tired to notice anything.

A boy about fourteen came to the door.

"May I ask who lives here?"

"My father."

"Will you tell me his name?"

"Deuteronomy Brown."

The name was music in my ears. It was like the sound of gurgling waters in a desert. It was soothing ointment to my bleeding spirits.

"Thank Heavens! At last!" I cried, as I almost sank to the floor.

D. B. appeared with a lamp in his hand. "Ah, my young friend. Why, I hardly knew you. You look weary. You should have telegraphed me you were coming. Walk in; you are welcome." He shook my hand as though I were a returned prodigal.

"Did you see your house as you came along? You passed right by it. Splendid place. Not a foothill farm in the section like it. Almost regret I parted with it; still, this place will do. You look tired. Sit down and rest yourself. My wife will get you some supper. You must rest to-night, and in the morning we'll go over your possessions. You will be pleased, delighted. It is a magnificent property. It will make you a splendid home."

I was not averse to resting. I had no desire to examine my property till morning. I had walked far enough. After supper I began to feel strong enough to talk, and so told my host of my experiences. He seemed very indignant.

"My young friend," he said, "you don't want to mix with the low, gossiping element here. You will be sure to get into trouble if you do. We have nothing to do with them. No Irish for us, if you please. That is the way they always do, We let them severely alone, and they won't be even courteous to strangers who are looking for us. I hope this will be a lesson to you. It won't do to have anything to do with these gossips. Why, they do nothing but run around from house to house talking about their neighbors We are something better than the common cattle around here, and we have found by sad experience that it won't do to mix with them. No sir."

My suspicions were confirmed. D. B. was not on friendly terms with his neighbors. But I was too tired to care about his neighbors. I fear I cared but very little about D. B. I was so weary that I even almost forgot what a benefactor to me he had been in giving me a chance to buy that fine farm adjoining his.

I was soon in my bed and asleep. Sleeping, I dreamed. But, oh, what dreams! Again the long tress of golden hair encircled my 160 acres of paradise. I saw the original of the miniature at my side, and we were sitting under a fig tree whispering words of love; then we seemed to be measuring for carpets; then we went out in front of the house, and I took a spade and dug a deep hole, and we planted the books on home decoration and landscape gardening, and then the fig tree seemed to change into something very like a thistle, and then the dear, sweet face by my side grew wrinkled and fierce, and it looked like the goat that disputed the trail with me, and as I looked more intently the face changed again and I thought it was the face of Deuteronomy Brown, and as I turned uneasily on my pillow I thought I heard him say, 'You must have nothing to do with the gossips;" and then all faded away. I might have slept till noon had not D. B. considerately called me. We breakfasted and I was ready to survey my possessions.

D. B. and I started out, and as we went along he spoke in glowing terms of my place. He showed me the beautiful flowers blooming in his yard, the young fruit trees that would bear next year, and the fine spring of clear, cold water.

"Now, my young friend, here we are; this is your southwest corner; the line runs up by my fence and over that hill, and takes in that fine manzanita bush on the brow of the hill. That is the finest bush of its kind around here. The whole hill slope was covered with these magnificent bushes. It was a beautiful sight; but somebody started a fire and they were all destroyed. I think it was some of those gossips. I had great difficulty in saving my fence—in fact it was burned in places. Now all your manzanita bushes are gone; but there is no small loss without a gain, if you look at it in a philosophical way. You won't have to clear the land. There is your house down there by the road, and behind it is the orchard. Just walk down and see the trees. See what a beautiful location for a home, right by the road, and all the hillslope for a background. The house used to be a hotel; that is why it is so near the road. There is the apple orchard—the oldest orchard around here."

So he went on describing one thing after another. I walked in silence. There was the beautiful hill slope. It was a hill slope sure enough. There was the hill and there the slope, and there were rocks; not one solid mass of rock, of course, that would have been useful had I wanted to start a granite qnarry; no, by no means a solid slope of rock, but just big granite bowlders, from the size of a man to that of a railroad car, standing around sort of negligent like, but standing on my land.

I walked toward the house. The doors and windows were gone. The building stood even with the road. If I laid out a front yard I would have to go back of the house to do so. The house was large, but part of the roof was gone. My first addition. would have to be doors, windows and a roof. I walked through the house. I would have to build a new floor. There had been a bannister on the stairs, but it had become tired of waiting for some one to use it, and had gone off some where. The house had been papered once, but the paper was mostly torn off. The cloth lining on which the paper had been fastened was gone from many of the rooms.

I went into the apple orchard. My mind was so pre-occupied that I did not say a word to D. B. I looked at the orchard. There were a few uncared-for trees that looked weary of waiting so long for some one to come and prune them. One tree had a few blossoms on it. I picked one and held it in my hand, lost in thought.

> 'Tis but a little fragrant flower;
> But, oh, how very dear;
> I press it in my clenched hand,
> And wish the fruit were here.

This was my place! This was my house! This was my orchard! This was the reality I had dreamed about for days! These were the rooms I was to measure for carpets! These the walls to decorate! That the place for the landscape garden! There the trees around which I was to build up a fruit farm! And all the books I had bought to aid me in these matters and the tape line were in my valise at "The Gap." This was the home I had thought of by day and dreamed of by night! This the place I was going to rebuild to make a fit abiding place for the original of the miniature! This was the fine foothill farm my benefactor D. B. had been so kind to let me buy before anyone else snatched it away!

I felt sad.

I turned to speak to D. B., but he was not there. I passed back through the house; he was not there. I went back to his house; he was not there. His wife told me he had been hastily called to Colfax, and had not had time to say good-bye, but he would be back by night. He had left word that he did not want to disturb my meditations as I examined my place. He thought I would be occupied during the day in planning changes and improvements, and had wanted me to feel perfectly at home.

I walked around. I examined my place more carefully. I was looking for any land that might not have become mixed up with the rocks. I glanced over the surrounding country. There certainly was no place like mine any where around; D. B. had told me so. He spoke the truth, the whole truth, and nothing but the truth. I had all the rocks in sight. Those rocks must have called a convention and gone on my place to hold it. There was a pretty fair fence around the place. I had paid D. B. for repairs on the fence when I bought the place. As I was taking a walk around my farm I met an intelligent young man. I hesitated to speak to him at first, fearing he might be one of the gossips; but I must talk to some one; I wanted information, and D. B. had been called away unexpectedly.

The young man and I became quite well acquainted. I told him my experience. He did not seem surprised. He only said:

"Old D. B.—we call him 'Deadbeat' around here—has done you up. He has been trying to sell that part of his place for two years. He lived in the house awhile and then built the one where you slept last night. He took the doors and windows and stair railing and everything else he could to use in his new house. I think he even took the cotton off the walls to use under the paper in his new house. I saw him move the pump. He had a young orchard, but took up all the trees he could move."

"I will prosecute him for taking my property," I interrupted.

"When did you buy the place?"

"Three weeks ago."

"Well, you can't do anything about that. He took all these things last fall."

"But I will prosecute him for selling me such a place."

"What good will that do? You say he told you there wasn't another place like it in the country, didn't you?"

"His very words "

"Well, there isn't. This is the poorest land, has the most rocks, and generally speaking is the very worst place you can find in Placer county. You should have examined it before buying."

I thought the matter over. I had nothing to do but accept a bad bargain.

"Tell you what I'll do," said my new acquaintance. "I've got a lot of goats. I'll pasture them on your land, and when the feed gets short you can bet your boots . they will get over old D. B.'s fence and eat things there."

"It's a go," I said; I was in a revengeful mood. "Pasture your goats on my place as long as you want. Get all the goats you can. Borrow some if you haven't enough. Fill up all the space between the rocks with goats. Here, I will write you an authority to use my place till I want it."

I did so. We parted. I did not wait to say good-bye to D. B. What was the use? I walked back to the railroad station. On the way I met the old goat that had disputed the path with me the night before. He recognized me and quietly stepped one side to let me pass. As he did so I thought I noticed a smile on his face.